What is a paragra

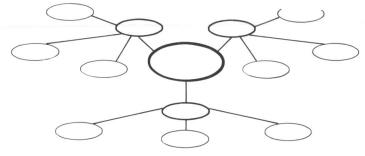

Discuss the parts of a paragraph with your students to be sure they understand the parts that it must contain. (A main idea expressed in a topic sentence with additional sentences providing supporting details.)

Read sample paragraphs to your students (in small groups or with the total class). Have them locate the topic sentence each time. You may use material from text or literature books or samples from your students' own work. Here are some examples to start with.

Arnie takes good care of his pet fish. He keeps his bowl filled with fresh water. He feeds them every morning. He keeps his cat away from the bowl. He takes the fish to the vet if they get sick.

Maria had an interesting job. Every day she and her monkey named Minkey would go to the city park. Maria would play lively music on her banjo while Minkey danced. People would gather around, laughing and clapping. After his dance, Minkey would hold out his hat and chatter until money was dropped into the hat.

I carry out the trash on Monday morning. I help my dad weed the garden. I make my bed and keep my bedroom tidy. I help my sister with the dinner dishes. Boy, do I have a lot of work to do every week!

1

Note: This page is too difficult for most second graders. The lesson is designed for two children to work on together. Each child determines the topic sentences independently, then compares the answers with his/her partner and explains why he/she chose those answers.

What's the Big Idea?

Read each paragraph carefully. Underline the main idea of each paragraph. Explain to your partner why you chose each answer.

Max's little sister can be a pest. For example, yesterday she drew all over his homework with marking pens. While he was at school she messed up the puzzle he had been working on for days. Then at dinner, she knocked her glass of milk over and it landed in his lap. Max was really mad!

Many changes happen to a caterpillar as it grows. It gets bigger and bigger as it eats leaves. One day it forms a fuzzy cocoon. After several weeks, a moth crawls out of the cocoon. It flies away when its wings are dry.

When a whale calf is hungry, it bumps its mother. She squirts milk into the calf's mouth. It drinks many gallons of milk in a short time. The milk is so rich a calf can gain eight pounds (four kilograms) in one hour. Eating this way the baby whale grows very fast.

Bonus: Write your own paragraph using this topic sentence.

"My sister (or brother) can really be a pest."

Give at least three reasons.

                   Paragraph Writing

Note: This page is too difficult for most second graders. The lesson is designed for two children to work on together. Each child determines the topic sentences independently, then compares answers with his/her partner and explains why he/she chose those answers.

What's the Big Idea?

Read each paragraph carefully. Underline the main idea of each paragraph. Explain to your partner why you chose each answer.

Disneyland is an exciting place to visit. First, you can go on many thrilling rides. Second, you can eat all kinds of good food. I like hot dogs and frozen bananas best. Next, there are many shows to see. Finally, you can watch a great parade before you go back home. You'll be tired, but happy.

Each day at 6:00 a.m., Kim puts on old clothes and heads for the barn. She must take care of her horse, General, before she goes to school. She carries a bucket of fresh water to his stall. Then she gets a pail of grain and an armload of alfalfa hay and puts it in his trough. Finally, she takes General to the pasture where he will graze while she is at school.

As the sun begins to disappear below the horizon, the sky starts to change colors. Bright pink clouds fill the sky, becoming darker as the sun sinks lower. The waves reflect the changing colors as they break along the shore. Sunsets are so beautiful by the sea.

Bonus: Write your own paragraph using this topic sentence.
"_____ is an exciting place to visit."
Include two or more reasons in your paragraph.

---

3   Paragraph Writing

What's My Topic Sentence?

This is an oral activity (for a small group or your entire class) to help children realize that there can be more than one appropriate topic sentence to fit a set of information.

1. wash your face
   brush your teeth
   comb your hair
   get dressed
   eat breakfast

2. built a nest
   laid eggs in the nest
   sat on the eggs
   gathered food for the hungry babies

3. built a sand castle
   ran in and out of the waves
   explored the tide pools
   roasted hot dogs over a fire

4. warm sunshine
   water
   fertilizer
   keep free of harmful insects

5. surveyor
   farmer
   general
   first president

6. gather the ingredients
   spread peanut butter on one slice of bread
   put jelly on the other slice
   put the pieces together
   eat it with a glass of cold milk

Have each student select one group of details. Use one of the topic sentences suggested by the group. Write a paragraph including the information given.

Using Paragraph Patterns

Many children have difficulty with the concept of writing a paragraph that truly contains one main idea. It is helpful to set a pattern or form to follow in the early stages of writing to help ensure success.

Pages 6 through 26 contain sample patterns that you might use. You may need to do some of the forms as guided lessons with your class if they are just beginning to write paragrpahs. Children who have had more writing experience and older students may be able to use the forms independently. Each page also contains a bonus activity. You will find patterns that can be used for the following types of paragraphs:

- Descriptive Paragraphs — Creating Word Pictures
- Writing Directions — "How to ..."
- Narrative Paragraphs — Tell a Story
- Paragraphs that Explain

1. Give each child a copy of the forms. (Or write the steps clearly on the chalkboard.)

2. Go through the steps required in the assignment.

   Brainstorming possible ideas is a crucial part of helping; your students will be prepared to put ideas down on paper. This is especially important with beginning writers.

3. Allow ample time for your students to write and rewrite. (Encourage interactions with classmates as they work on rewriting for clarity.)

5   Paragraph Writing

Lunch Time

I hate to find _____ in my lunch.

_____

- -

(Describe how it looks.)

- -

- -

(Describe how it tastes.)

- -

It makes me want to -

_____

Bonus: Write another paragraph about what you hate to find on the breakfast table. Follow the same pattern you just practiced.

Take a crayon and underline your topic sentence.

- -

_____

- -

_____

- -

_____

- -

_____

- -

Let's Eat

The very best food in the world is _____
_____
_____
(Describe how it looks.) _____
_____
(Describe how it smells.) _____
_____
(Describe how it tastes.) _____
_____
_____
_____ You should try it some time. I'll bet you like it too.
_____

Bonus: Write a paragraph about your favorite dessert, snack, party food, or sandwich.

Describe how it looks, smells, and tastes. Explain why you think someone else should try it.

_____
_____
_____
_____
_____
_____
_____
_____
_____
_____
_____
_____

What a Noise!

Pet stores are very noisy places. _____

_____

_____

(Give three examples of how noisy it is.)

_____

_____

_____

The next time I go there I will _____

_____

_____

Bonus: Write about a quiet place. Give three ways you can tell how quiet it is.

Don't forget to indent.

_____

_____

_____

_____

_____

Unusual Places

If you could see under my bed, you would be amazed! The first

thing you would notice is _____

_____

_____

Next, _____

_____

_____ Finally, _____

You would probably say _____

_____

Now, tell me what it's like under your bed.

Bonus: Write about another unusual place someone could look. Use this topic
sentence to get you started.

Follow the same pattern you just practiced.
Put a green dot by each of your supporting sentences.

If you could see in my _____

_____

_____, you would be amazed!

_____

_____

_____

_____

_____

                                       Paragraph Writing

I'm So Excited

Have you ever been so excited you felt like you would burst if you

didn't tell someone what had happened? I felt that way when _____

_____

_____

_____

So I ran to tell _____ because _____

_____

_____

_____

Bonus: Describe a time when you felt lonely. You may follow the pattern above or try to write the paragraph on your own.

Remember to use one topic sentence and two or more supporting detail sentences.

_____

_____

_____

_____

_____

_____

_____

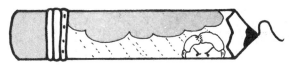 **What a Miserable Day**

Yesterday was the worst day of my life. I felt awful. It started off when

_____

_____

_____

_____

Then _____

_____

_____

The last straw was when _____

_____

_____

Tomorrow has got to be better.

Bonus: Write a paragraph about one of the feelings listed below. Describe how you felt and why you felt that way.

_____

_____

_____

_____

_____

_____

_____

_____

_____

_____

_____

frightened   embarrassed   cheerful   silly

My Best Friend

Can you guess who my best friend is? She/He _ _ _ _ _ _ _ _ _ _ _ _ _ _ _ _

_ (looks like) _ _ _ _ _ _ _ _ _

_ _

She/He can _

(talents and abilities)

_ _

I can always count on her/him to _

_ _

If you guessed _ you are right!

Bonus: Write three supporting detail sentences explaining why this person is your hero.

Remember to indent your paragraph.

Use this topic sentence.

My hero is _

_ _

_ _

_ _

_ _

_ _

_ _

Presidents

Although George Washington and Abraham Lincoln were both presidents

of the United States, their lives were very different. _ _ _ _ _ _ _ _ _ _ _ _ _ _ _

(Give two or more examples.)

_ _

_ _

_ _

_ _

I think the biggest difference was _

_ _

Bonus: Give two or more examples.
Circle your supporting sentences.
Use this as your topic sentence.

Although George Washington and Abraham Lincoln lived at different times, their lives

were similar in many ways. _

_ _

_ _

_ _

_ _

_ _

How to Fix a Snack

I like to fix my own snack. Sometimes I make myself a ─ ─ ─ ─ ─ ─ ─ ─ ─ ─ ─ ─

─ ─ ─ ─ ─ ─ ─ ─ ─ ─ ─ ─ sandwich. First I ─ ─ ─ ─ ─ ─ ─ ─ ─ ─ ─ ─ ─ ─ ─ ─ ─

Second I ─

Third I ─

Last of all I ─

It tastes great with a large glass of ─ ─ ─ ─ ─ ─ ─ ─ ─ ─ ─ ─ ─ ─ ─ ─ ─ to drink.

Bonus: Draw a picture in each box to show what you
did first, second, third, and last of all.

Bath Time

You may think it is easy to give your pet a bath.   Not when it's my

_____   First I have to   _____

_____   _____

_____

Next I   _____

_____

Then I   _____

_____

Finally I   _____

_____   Now I need to take a bath myself!

Bonus: Pretend you have to feed porridge to your baby brother or sister.
You may use this topic sentence or write one of your own.
    You may think it is easy to feed a little baby.
Give at least three steps you have to follow.

_____

_____

_____

_____

_____

_____

_____

Artist at Work

There are certain steps I must follow when I want to paint a picture. First

I must get _____

_____ Second I _____

_____ Next I _____

_____

_____ Last of all I have to _____

_____

Bonus: Think of something else you like to make. List the steps you have to follow.
Remember:

      Topic sentence.
      Supporting details.
      Indent your paragraph.

_____

_____

_____

_____

_____

_____

By the Sea

Picnics at the beach are really fun. But you do have to plan carefully. This

is what I do. First I see if -

_____
(how you will get to the beach)

- -

Then I invite -

- -

- Finally, I pack a lunch of - - - - - - - - - - - - - - - - - - -

- -

By the way, don't forget to read the weather report! Have fun.

Bonus: Explain what you would do if it started to rain after you got to the beach. Underline your topic sentence.

Frogs

Frogs are very interesting animals. I like the way they look. - - - - - - -

_____

- -

(Tell about how they look.)

- -

Frogs can move in several ways. -

(Tell ways they move.)

- -

- -

The most interesting fact about frogs is - - - - - - - - - - - - - - - -

- -

- -

Bonus: Illustrate one of your paragraphs.

Bats and birds are alike in several ways. They both _ _ _ _ _ _ _ _ _ _ _ _ _ _ _
_____

They also _
_____

_ _
_____

Finally _
_____

_ _
_____

You can probably think of more ways they are the same.

Bonus: Now write a paragraph that explains how bats and birds are different.

Dinosaurs

In my opinion the most unusual dinosaur was ------------------

_____

- -

(Give three or more reasons.)

- -

_____

- -

_____

- -

_____

- -

_____

Bonus: Use one of these topic sentences to help you write another paragraph about an animal (living, extinct, or imaginary).

The most unusual animal I ever heard of was the _____

_____ is the most dangerous of all the animals.

I would really like to have a _____ for a pet.

If I were an animal I would want to be a _____

Give two or more reasons to explain why you feel this way.

- -

_____

- -

_____

- -

_____

- -

_____

- -

 Paragraph Writing

My best friend's _____ party was the most fun

I've ever had. Everyone had to _____

_____

Then we _____

_____

_____

Best of all was when _____

_____

_____

I didn't want the party to end.

Bonus: Use this topic sentence.

           It was the worst party I ever went to. I couldn't wait to go home.

      Give two or more reasons.

_____

_____

_____

_____

_____

_____

_____

_____

_____

_____

Note: Sometimes it helps to draw first, then write. You may want to make the bonus activity
a prewriting step for your students.

Spiders in the Bedroom

Herman saw a spider crawling across the ceiling of his bedroom.   It was

_____

- -

_____

Herman felt -

_____

- -

_____

He decided to -

_____

- -

_____

_____

- -

Bonus: In the first box draw the spider.
In the second box draw Herman's face when he saw the spider.
In the third box show what Herman decided to do.

The Mysterious

_____

Kelly found an unusual _____ on the way home

from school. When she started to rub the dirt off of the _____

_____, strange things began to happen. First she noticed _____

_____ Then _____

_____ But the strangest thing was when _____

_____

_____

Bonus: Use this paragraph as the start of a longer story about Kelly

and her unusual _____

_____

_____

_____

_____

_____

_____

_____

_____

_____

Planet X

When the first manned space ship landed on Planet X, the explorers were not prepared for what they found. As soon as they stepped off the ship they noticed

_____

_____

_____

_____ And then

_____

they _____

_____

_____

The most exciting discovery was _____

_____

_____

Bonus: Illustrate Planet X showing what the astronauts found there.

"Safe" Topic Sentences

Some children have difficulty getting started on independent paragraph writing. It can be helpful in the beginning to provide them with "safe" topic sentences. As they become more experienced writers and meet with success, they can begin to move on to develop their own more specific main idea sentences. Here is a selection that can be used with beginning writers. Add the appropriate subject to the models below.

- Let me tell you about _____.

- Have you ever wondered about _____?

- Have you ever wondered why _____?

- I like to _____ for many reasons.

- I know how to _____. First...

- I just learned these facts about _____.

- I think _____ was a very brave person for these reasons. (You can substitute other characteristics such as creative, dangerous, foolish, etc.)

- Let me tell you how _____ and _____ are different (or alike).

- Many changes happen to _____ as they grow. First...

- It is fun to _____. You...

- People used to think _____ but now we know...

- _____ is like...

Note: Here is an organizational method third and fourth graders can use when they are writing a story or report requiring more than one paragraph.

Planning My Paragraphs — Outlining

Select a subject and think of two or more important things you want to say about the subject. These become the main ideas for your paragraphs. Use the outline as you write your paragraphs.

Subject of the Report

1. **Main idea**

    a. supporting detail

    b. supporting detail

    c. supporting detail

2. **Main idea**

    a. supporting detail

    b. supporting detail

    c. supporting detail

Etc.

My Pet Dog

1. **What she looks like**

    a. brown and white spots

    b. long, straight hair

    c. wet, shiny nose

2. **What she can do**

    a. fetch a stick

    b. bring in the newspaper

    c. protect the house

3. **How I take care of her**

    a. feed her every day

    b. see that she has a clean place to sleep

    c. give her a bath when she needs one

    d. play with her every day

How to make a Sandwich

1. **Collect what you will need**

    a. bread, peanut butter, jelly

    b. knife

2. **Steps to follow**

    a. first — open the jars

    b. second — open the bread

    c. next — spread the stuff

    d. then — put the pieces together

    e. last of all — eat it up

Paragraph Writing

Note: Reproduce this form for children to use when writing a multi-paragraph report or story.

_____
subject

1. _____

   a. _____

   b. _____

   c. _____

2. _____

   a. _____

   b. _____

   c. _____

3. _____

   a. _____

   b. _____

   c. _____

Get a sheet of paper. Take these notes and use them as a guide as you write your paragraphs.

27 Paragraph Writing

Planning My Paragraphs — A Simple Web

- Select a subject and write it in the large oval.

- Think of two or more important things you want to say about the subject. Write these ideas in the middle-size ovals. These are your main ideas for each paragraph.

- Put supporting information for each main idea in the small ovals.

Paragraph Writing

Note: Reproduce this form for children to use when writing multi-paragraph reports or stories.

Take a sheet of paper and use these notes to guide you as you write your paragraphs.

main idea

subject

main idea

main idea

Preparing a Paragraph

1. Select the subject of your paragraph.

2. Decide what the main idea of the paragraph will be.

3. Think about what you want to tell in this paragraph. Create a topic sentence that gets the main idea across to your readers.

4. Add details to your paragraph. Think...does each detail sentence support the main idea?

5. Reread your paragraph. Can you see ways to change it to make it better?

6. Proof your paragraph. (You may want to ask a friend to proof it also.) Check:

   _____ I indented the first word.

   _____ I used correct punctuation marks.

   _____ My paragraph says what I wanted it to say.

7. Copy your paragraph in your best handwriting.

8. Share it with a classmate.

         Paragraph Writing

Paragraph Writing Center

Set aside a section of a bulletin board and a small table. Put directions for how to use the center on the bulletin board. Add pockets made from manilla envelopes (see illustration). Use these pockets to hold:

Sentence strips to be placed in correct order to form a paragraph. (Put in one or two sentences that do not belong if you want to make the task more difficult.)

Cards containing paragraph patterns (use any of the patterns from pages 6 through 26) or topic sentences (see page 32 and inside back cover for ideas) for the children to select.

Magazines that can be cut up. Children can use the pictures when writing descriptive paragraphs or short stories.

A supply of writing and drawing paper.

Push pins in the bulletin board so children can display their final paragraphs.

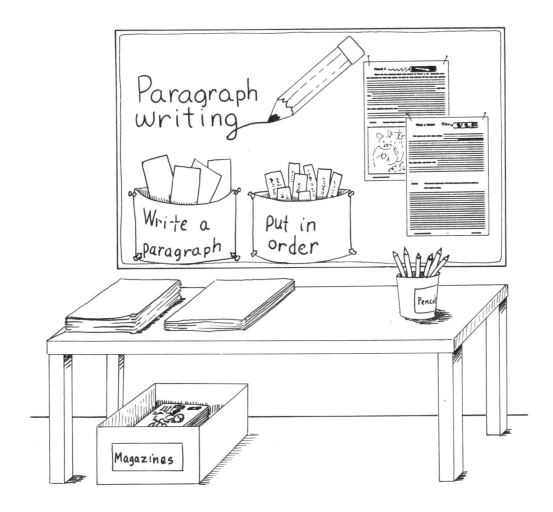

Note: Place these topic sentences on tag strips to use in the writing center described on page 31.

I love to eat _____ more than anything else in the world.

I saw the strangest sight on the way to school today.

Rain makes me feel _____ for many reasons.

Did you ever notice how much _____ and _____ are alike?

_____ is the most exciting game to play.

I have really changed since I was six. Then I... Now I...

I just read an interesting book about _____. I learned...

The worst book I ever read was _____. I didn't like it for these reasons.

 Paragraph Writing